Abigail
Eats Bugs

by Virginia Pye

Abigail Eats Bugs
Copyright © 2018 by Virginia Pye

All rights reserved. No part of this publication may be reproduced, distributed, or transmitted in any form or by any means, including photocopying, recording, or other electronic or mechanical methods, without the prior written permission of the author, except in the case of brief quotations embodied in critical reviews and certain other non-commercial uses permitted by copyright law.

Tellwell Talent
www.tellwell.ca

ISBN
978-0-2288-0174-0 (Hardcover)
978-0-2288-0173-3 (Paperback)

Thanks so much to my family for their encouragement:
Bud, Laura, Jason, Laurie Ann and Greg

One summer day, Griffin and Grace were walking home through a big green field. Suddenly, Griffin spotted something among the flowers.

"Grace, Grace! Quick, come see!" he yelled.

"Griffin, if it's another bug —"

"Yes, it is, but it's special. It has a dress like your favorite one. It's red with black spots."

"Okay," Grace said, smiling at her twin brother.

"Oh, how pretty!" Grace could not take her eyes off of Griffin's new polka-dotted find sitting on a leaf.

"Yes, she *is* pretty," Griffin said, jumping up and down. He was sure he had found a special bug. Never before had he seen a bug with such beautiful colors. "What should we name her?"

Before Grace could answer, a tiny voice squeaked out: "My name is Abigail … and I am *not* a bug!!!"

Abigail jumped off the leaf and quickly unfolded her wings. She flew in front of the twins' startled faces. Grace screamed.

"Are you okay?" Griffin asked his sister.

"Yes, I'm fine," Abigail said, again before Grace could answer. "Takes more than that to scare me."

She landed on the ground, fluttering her wings. "See, I have two set of wings. The outer set is the hard shell for protection, and the inner set is what I use to fly."

"What are you?" asked Grace, no longer frightened.

"I'm a beetle, but most people call me a ladybug."

"A ladybug?" said both twins at the same time.

"Yes!" Abigail said, taking a little bow. "And I have a very important job! I am a gardener's best friend. I am here to keep your gardens clean of mites."

"What's a mite?" asked Grace.

"Well, for one thing, it's very tasty," said Abigail. The twins both made "grossed-out" faces.

Abigail giggled, then said, "A mite is a tiny, soft-bodied insect that feeds on plants. Mites suck plant juices out of the stems and roots, which is not good for the plants. I eat the mites so you and your family can enjoy the vegetables and flowers." She beamed with pride. "So, let's go get something *more* to eat!"

Off they went. With Abigail perched on Griffin's shoulder, the twins rode their bikes around all the gardens in their neighbourhood.

"STOP, STOP!" Abigail yelled. "Look at these roses, so beautiful: yellow, pink, red … and the smell. AHHH, just like sugar, so sweet!"

She flew off Griffin's shoulder and landed on the first rose stem. She started to eat the mites on it.

"Yuck! What are you doing?" asked Grace.

"I'm hungry!" Abigail said and smiled. Bits of mites were stuck between her teeth. She let out a loud burp. Griffin could not stop laughing.

"Remember?" Abigail said as she chewed. "This keeps the plants healthy."

Abigail explained how she is better for gardens than a chemical pesticide. "I can eat up to 50 mites off of the plants with no damage done!"

"That's a lot of mites," said Grace, impressed.

"We need to find the best gardens so I can *really* do my job!" said Abigail.

"Okay," Griffin said. "Grace, we could go to Flower Pot Lane, where your friend Chloe lives. They have a big garden, and while we are there I can play with her brother, Aiden."

"Can we, please?" asked Abigail, with huge eyes and a wide grin.

"Sure," said Grace. "It would be nice to see Chloe too."

Along Flower Pot Lane, the front yards were filled with colorful flowers of all shapes and sizes. Each back yard had its own vegetable garden, but Chloe's garden was the biggest.

"WOWEE!" Abigail was flying around with her large brown eyes bulging out. "I can't believe this!! I'm in ladybug paradise."

The gardens were the best Abigail had ever seen. "I will *definitely* get some work done here," she said, licking her lips. The twins went off to find Chloe and Aiden.

Grace and Griffin returned with their friends to help Abigail with the rest of the garden work. They pulled all the weeds, pruned the fruit tree, and watered the flowers, tomatoes, and carrots.

Grace, Griffin, and Abigail spent the entire summer together. They had a great time helping out in the gardens of all their friends and neighbors. Abigail lived up to her name as a gardener's best friend. That summer, Flower Pot Lane had the most beautiful gardens anyone had ever seen.

While sitting under a tree one day at the end of summer, Griffin said to Abigail, "You're growing up and getting bigger."

Abigail smiled. "Yes, Griffin, I'm getting ready for the winter. I need to have lots of fat on me to make it through hibernation."

"What's hibernation?" asked Grace.

"It's when I sleep all winter long because it's too cold for me to stay outside. Sleep helps me to build up energy to help the gardens next spring."

"Where will you sleep?" asked Griffin.

"I'll find a nice warm spot with other ladybugs in tree bark or a leaf pile, or maybe even in a roof," Abigail said, starting to yawn.

"We'll miss you," said Grace, and Griffin nodded.

"And I'll miss you both," Abigail said, yawning again. "Well, I better go before I get too tired to find a good spot. See you next spring!"

As the twins waved goodbye, Abigail flew off to find her bed.

Manufactured by Amazon.ca
Bolton, ON